MEDIEVAL CHRISTMAS

Medieval Christmas | Toni Mount

Christmas in the Middle Ages was celebrated with as much joy and enthusiasm as it is today, perhaps even more. Discover the origins of our modern traditions and how people would celebrate Christmas without turkey, tinsel or Santa Claus.

MEDIEVAL CHRISTMAS

The Origins and Traditions of Christmas in the Middle Ages

Toni Mount

Cover image: Adoration of the Magi from the Book of Hours of Rene of Anjou, Egerton 1070 f.34v BL

Frontispiece: Les très riches heures du Jean Duc de Berry (Ms. 65) – Musée Condé à Chantilly, France

Copyright © 2025 by Toni Mount

ISBN: 978-0-9555925-7-7

All rights reserved. No part of this book may be reproduced in any manner whatsoever without written permission except in the case of brief quotations embodied in critical articles and reviews.

First Printed October 2025

Published by Echoes from History
An imprint of author, Toni Mount

www.tonimount.com

Contents	Page
Ch 1 The Origins of Christmas	7
Ch 2 Food and Feasting	17
Ch 3 Mysteries, Miracles and Mummers	32
Ch 4 The Twelve Days of Christmas	43
Ch 5 The Spirit of Christmas Giving	55
Ch 6 Echoes of Joy	63
Ch 7 Old Man Winter, Saint Nicholas and Father Christmas	72
Table of Images	82
Index	84
Meet the Author	86
Also by Toni Mount	87

Chapter 1 – The Origins of Christmas

1. Bringing home the evergreens

From Pagan Rites to Christian Tradition

Today, Christmas is a global celebration filled with lights, trees and gifts. It's a time for families to come together, sharing good food, merriment and entertainment. At least, that's the intention.

However, the roots of Christmas lie in a rich blend of ancient pagan customs, early Christian adaptation and even royal influences. Long before it became a mainstream Christian holiday, Midwinter – around the 21st of December, when daylight hours are at their shortest in the northern hemisphere – was a time of important cultural and spiritual observance across Europe with traditions that still affect how we mark the season today.

The Winter Solstice

Before Christianity spread through Britain, Midwinter was already a spiritually significant time for pagan communities. As long ago as the Neolithic Period, the famous circle of Stonehenge was constructed with reference to the Winter Solstice, the longest night of the year. This was the symbolic point marking the turning of the seasons, when darkness began to give way to the light. Ancient peoples honoured this moment of the sun's returning with festivals that included fire, feasting and the worship of Nature deities associated with renewal, rebirth and fertility. In the cold, dark days of winter, it was wise to remind the sun that the earth was waiting and it had work to do, warming and reviving the bleak land.

2. Old Man Winter

In the Anglo-Saxon period in England, they celebrated the winter festival of Yule which lasted about ten days, from 21st December to 1st January. The Vikings had *Jul*. Yule seems to have covered a number of pagan celebrations including the god Woden's Wild Hunt through the skies and *Modraniht* or 'Mothers' Night' on 24th December, a celebration of all females, whether goddesses, mortal women or animals – a connection to ancient fertility rites. Folklore abounds and its origins are obscure but it seems the Yule log was as large as would fit the hearth and was put on the fire to burn, hopefully, for the ten days of Yuletide, providing light and heat in the darkest, cold days when the sun gave little of either.

The traditional character of Old Man Winter reflected the season's dual nature: harsh and merry, dangerous yet celebratory. This fellow, a forerunner of today's Father Christmas – as opposed to Santa Claus who was very different – represented the unpredictable power of winter. He was portrayed as a club-wielding visitor demanding food, drink and hospitality in exchange for bringing good cheer and merriment to his hosts. And woe betide anyone who didn't join in the fun: he would beat them with his club until they did. Throughout history, giving food and shelter to travellers has always been regarded as a charitable act, the more so in harsh winter weather. The idea was that generosity to others would be rewarded by surviving the lean times and seeing spring return once more.

These longstanding customs of Nature worship, recalling the sun and the tradition of Old Man Winter posed a challenge for the early Church. Pagan celebrations were deeply rooted in daily life and any outright bans would not only have offended folk but the possibility of upsetting any turbulent and fickle gods would have been terrifying to them. Such actions could alienate any potential converts to Christianity. Instead, wise Church leaders employed a more strategic approach: adaptation.

Christian Conversion and the Birth of Christmas

Christianity was made the official religion of the Roman Empire in c.313 AD, but the Romans already had an entire universe of pagan gods. Being forced to acknowledge that there was but one God was not going to be popular if they had to give up all the celebrations honouring those many gods and like other pagan religions, the Romans had an especially riotous festival around the midwinter solstice known as Saturnalia. In praise of the god Saturn, lord of agriculture and crops, it reminded him that it was time he returned to make the earth fertile once more.

3. Celebrating Roman Saturnalia

The occasion consisted of a week or more of too much wine, an excess of food and an orgy of sex – how better to encourage fertility?

Needless to say, any attempt to forbid or eliminate these popular solstice festivities would not be well received by folk who wanted to liven up those depressing dreary days.

> **Did you know?** Mistletoe – *Viscum album* – is a small semi-parasitic evergreen shrub which forms large spherical balls up to a metre wide in the tops of trees. Its leaves, stems and white berries are all poisonous. It used to be held sacred by the Celtic Druids because it seemed to grow magically without roots or any connection to the ground. It is supposed that the Druid priests cut it down with a golden sickle and caught it in a white sheet so the earth never touched this sacred plant which belonged to the gods. Because mistletoe flourishes in midwinter and is far more visible when most trees are bare, it became associated with the solstice festivals, especially as a symbol of fertility. Each berry represented a sexual act so our idea of kissing under the mistletoe is a very pale version of the Celtic rite. Traditionally, a berry should be removed for each kiss – or whatever you will. Because of its sexual associations, it was forbidden to take mistletoe into a church at Christmas.

So, instead, the Church repurposed these festivities. It established 25th December as the official date to celebrate the birth of God's son, Jesus Christ – despite there being no biblical evidence for this timing – aligning it with the existing midwinter festival. This overlap allowed new converts to keep their familiar traditions and recognise Christian teachings. Pagan magic became Almighty God's miracles. In this way, Christmas never was a purely religious observance but more of a hybrid occasion. By merging seasonal customs with a theological event, it allowed communities to convert from paganism to

Christianity with less distress and fear of offending the old gods. Where conflict did arise, it was most often because Christian morals could not be seen to approve the excesses of the celebrations nor the more blatant sexual activities of the accompanying fertility rites.

On Christmas Eve, the pagan tradition of decorating the house with evergreens continued as before. The idea of 'Decking the hall with boughs of holly' is an ancient one, though the carol is more modern. People wrapped up warm and went out into the woods, fields and hedgerows. Men gathered holly, its spiky leaves representing the male as defender of the family. Women picked ivy with its softer leaves and clinging stems representing the gentler female binding the family together. Churches were also decorated with holly, its gender-specific symbolism set aside as it was now associated with Christ's crown of thorns and the red berries a reminder of the blood he shed for mankind. Ivy garlands were draped about the font where babies were baptised into the Christian faith, to be nurtured and held safe within the Christian family. Together with yew boughs for longevity, these were the favoured Christmas evergreens but mistletoe was not permitted in a church, unable to shake off its earlier pagan significance.

The First Christian Christmas in England – 597 AD

The now-Christian Romans had left these shores in 410 AD and many who remained slipped back into paganism. Also, the Anglo-Saxons had come to stay, bringing their own gods with them – Woden, Thunor (Thor), etc. So, in 597 AD, Augustine – a future saint – arrived from Rome with a small group of monks, bringing Christianity back to

England, landing on the shore of the Anglo-Saxon Kingdom of Kent. King Aethelberht was already familiar with this religion and its single God because his wife was a Christian so it didn't take Augustine long to persuade the king to convert. Aethelberht was baptised on Whitsunday, 597, and ordered a mass baptism of his people on Christmas Day that same year. While this may have been a sincere personal religious conversion, it was also a clever political strategy. For many Anglo-Saxons, following the king's lead in religious matters was a wise precaution and made practical sense – even if some continued to honour gods like Woden privately. Hedging your bets was common as people tried to reconcile the new faith with their old beliefs. But from the king's point of view, Christianity offered something important: divine sanction for their rule. The Anglo-Saxon gods said nothing about kings but the Bible's Old Testament in particular reinforced the idea of rulers chosen and blessed by God. This gave religious support for monarchy with not only divine approval but the threat of divine wrath against those who opposed it.

King Aelfred makes Christmas official

4. Anglo-Saxon King and Queen

By the late ninth century, under King Aelfred the Great, Christianity had become the official religion of the land. Aelfred ruled from 871 to 899 AD and passed legislation declaring that 'Middewinter', a now-Christian festival beginning on 25th December, should be observed with twelve days of rest and celebration. A great idea for the wealthy but more difficult to uphold for their servants and lesser folk.

Though the term 'Christmas' – or more correctly 'Christ's Mass' – wasn't yet fully established, the festive period was now officially recognised as sacred. Aelfred also introduced an extended religious break for Easter, ensuring that even commoners could participate in the most significant Christian observances. Importantly, Aelfred promoted literacy and the translation of religious texts into Old English, making the Gospels more accessible to ordinary people. These efforts helped to embed Christianity not just in law, but in daily life.

His legal reforms also had a social dimension. He declared that seasonal provisions must be made for slaves, including food, meat and gifts at Christmas and Easter. Female slaves were entitled to slightly less than males but still received aid as society was increasingly shaped by Christian values – especially of charity during festive periods.

Guthrum's Attack and the Perils of Celebration

Despite these advances, Christmas in early medieval England was not always a time of peace. In 878 AD, the Viking leader, Guthrum, launched a surprise attack on Chippenham, one of King Aelfred's residences in his Kingdom of Wessex, during the Epiphany celebration on 6th January. At that moment, Christian nobles and military leaders were likely to be busy feasting, drinking and observing religious rites. The date chosen for the attack was no coincidence. The Vikings, though pagan, were well aware of the major Christian festivals. The occasions were predictable and distracted those who took part, giving their enemies an opportunity to strike while leaders were otherwise engaged. Guthrum's plan aimed to catch Aelfred off guard and end the resistance of the Kingdom of Wessex in a bloodbath. Fortunately, Aelfred wasn't at Chippenham at the time and the plan failed. But this episode highlights the vulnerability created by Christian communal celebration; that it could expose weaknesses in a society structured around a fixed religious calendar.

> **Did You Know?** King Raedwald of East Anglia is thought to have been the occupant of the famous and fabulous Sutton Hoo burial ship, uncovered in the mid-twentieth century. Raedwald was a contemporary of King Aethelberht of Kent and, despite his obviously pagan burial, there were definite hints of Christian rites, including a set of silver spoons decorated with crosses. Was Raedwald ensuring his place in the afterlife, observing the worship of both the old gods and the new – just in case?

The Lasting Legacy

What we now recognise as Christmas evolved gradually – from solstice bonfires to solemn church rites, from pagan revellers to Christian kings, the celebration took shape. While later periods, particularly the Victorian era, would add further embellishments like Christmas trees, cards and Santa Claus, the foundations of the holiday had been laid by Aethelberht and Aelfred. These kings helped to establish Christmas as a religious and cultural fixture. Meanwhile, the Church's willingness to incorporate rather than destroy pagan traditions made Christianity more acceptable to converts.

Thus, Christmas as we know it is not a sudden invention but the product of centuries of change – a complex blend of belief, politics and festivity that reflects both the spiritual and earthly needs of society.

5. Winter Solstice at Stonehenge

Chapter 2 – Food & Feasting

6. Banquet of Richard II

Feasting at the Heart of Christmas

As we have heard, the idea of Christmas feasting has roots that stretch far back into pagan antiquity. Before it was the Christian celebration we know today, midwinter festivals like the Roman Saturnalia were held to mark the winter solstice. These were joyous occasions filled with merriment, food and drink – activities which later made their way into Christmas despite early Church disapproval.

As Christianity spread, Church leaders realised that these pagan customs were too deeply embedded and popular in society to be eradicated. Instead of suppressing them, they rebranded them. Saturnalia gradually morphed into

Christmas, the birth of Christ replacing sun-worship and fertility rites, while much of the feasting and celebration remained intact. This pragmatic approach allowed Christianity to flourish while maintaining the communal joy of winter festivities.

Royal Feasts and Political Theatre

By the medieval period, Christmas was an elaborate affair, especially at the royal court. King John in 1213 and his son Henry III in 1252 used Christmas feasts as both a celebration and an occasion for demonstrating political power. Both monarchs were unpopular at the time of these lavish gatherings and needed to showcase their wealth and royal generosity, reminding their belligerent barons not only of the king's authority but of his ability to provide on a huge scale and grant favour.

The royal Christmas feast was a spectacular event. Guests included high-ranking nobles, foreign ambassadors, important clerics and senior military commanders. The act of hosting these elites under one roof for extended celebrations, featuring music, entertainers and vast quantities of food and drink, helped the monarch maintain influence, bestow favour and forge alliances. Both friends and enemies were invited as all needed to be suitably impressed and feel they were indebted to the king. In John's case, it didn't work; in Henry's it was somewhat more successful for a while, at least.

Feasts for the People: Hospitality & Social Obligation

While kings and lords used feasts to display dominance, the tradition of generosity extended beyond politics.

Hospitality was considered a sacred duty, especially during the Christmas period. Lords were expected to open their halls to tenants and the less fortunate. These acts of charity provided a lifeline to peasants, who might otherwise suffer from hunger and cold. A simple gift of firewood was always welcome.

Even the poorest tenant could expect a share of the seasonal bounty. Bread, ale and some kind of meat – the latter a luxury for many during most of the year – were distributed from the lord's kitchens. Leftover food, extra ale and warm fires became expressions of feudal responsibility and reinforced the lord's communal ties with the villagers.

The Medieval Christmas Menu: Far from meagre Fare

Despite modern assumptions about medieval diets, Christmas fare was anything but plain. Both rich and poor indulged in the most elaborate meals of the year. Roasted meats, pies, sweetmeats and spiced wine were served in abundance. While lords dined on exotic delicacies, their tenants enjoyed simpler but still hearty fare, often served at the lower tables in the great hall.

The Court of Richard II enjoyed especially lavish feasts and not only at Christmas. Around 1390 Richard's cook – name unknown, sadly – compiled a recipe book of the king's favourite dishes which has survived to the present. Titled the *Forme of Cury* it is based upon a vast three course meal, each course including roasted meats, sweet dishes and ending with a 'subtlety'. The first course alone included boar's heads, venison, roasted swans and a sort of custard tart containing dried fruit and parsley. A subtlety was a huge confection of sugar paste and marzipan (imagine a wedding cake, without the cake) modelled in the shape of a castle, a dragon, a ship or some other amazing device often complete with fireworks.

> **Did you know?** There was a luxurious medieval dish called 'Blank-Mang' or 'white food'. It was made with chopped, cooked chicken, blanched almonds and rice cooked together in almond milk with lard, sugar and salt added. Once the rice was cooked, the blancmange was served garnished with sugared anise and fried almonds. Based on a recipe from the *Forme of Cury* and so different from modern blancmange. Almonds, sugar, rice and anise spice were all expensive imports

Christmas was a time of both religious and social revelry. The Church's attempts to enforce solemnity were often overshadowed by games, music and communal fun. Having a good time was not only tolerated but expected; joy and goodwill were believed to bring good fortune.

The Evolution of the Mince Pie

One of the most enduring Christmas dishes is the mince pie, though its medieval version differed greatly from today's sweet treat. Originally called the 'Christmas Pie', it was a large, meaty centrepiece and meant to be shared. Filled with off-cuts of beef, mutton, goose or chicken, along with suet, dried fruit and spices, it was more savoury than sweet. The meats were the less attractive bits off the roasts, not elegant enough to be served at table.

The salt-crust pastry shell – referred to as a 'coffin' or, at Christmas, as a 'cradle' – was thick and not meant to be eaten, simply serving as a container for the ingredients.

Sometimes shaped to resemble a cradle and adorned with a figure of Baby Jesus, modelled in pastry, and often gilded with gold leaf, these pies were symbolic as well as practical. Eating the Christmas Pie was a ritual: the lid with the gilded Baby was lifted off – never cut with a knife as this would bring bad luck.

7. A Medieval Christmas Pie

The youngest child present received the first spoonful and made a wish, then everybody was served, eating the mixture with spoons until the pastry case was empty and disposable – no washing up required.

The spices added two elements to the dish. Firstly, the huge cost of these exotic ingredients demonstrated the host's wealth and access to luxuries from distant lands. Secondly, spices carried symbolic weight, representing the gifts of the Magi or the Three Kings as presented to the Christ Child. Gold – regarded as a culinary spice could appear, literally, in the form of gilded pies; frankincense was represented by aromatic spices like cinnamon, and myrrh was symbolised by warming alternatives such as ginger. These ingredients elevated the dish into a celebration of both the sacred and the extravagant.

> **Did You Know?** The gold leaf used to gild pies, meatballs and to make other dishes look more impressive, is edible but it passes through the body, undigested and undamaged. Ultimately, it ends up in the latrine pit. In medieval times, folk known as 'dong-famers' were paid to empty the latrine pits and any valuables found – from finger rings to weapons – were the perks of the job. The fragments of gold leaf from the fine food were collected up, washed – hopefully – and sold to the goldsmith to be melted down and reused. You never know where that gold locket has been in the past!

Brawn and Boar: The role of Meat in festive Celebrations

A roasted boar's head was the centrepiece of noble Christmas tables, a tradition introduced by the Romans and Vikings. In both cultures, the boar was an animal of significance, hunted and sacrificed during winter festivals. Decorated with garlands, the boar's head came to symbolise courage and abundance.

8. The Boar's Head presented by the Steward

Queens' College, Oxford, helped to enshrine the boar's head in Christmas lore and to this day, the college hosts an annual mid-winter feast known as the Boar's Head Gaudy, accompanied by a special carol. The event is so popular it is restricted to a certain number of old college members.

The Boar's Head Carol

The boar's head in hand bear I,
Bedecked with bays and rosemary;
And I pray you, my masters, be merry,
Quo testis in convivio *(So many as are here together)*
Refrain:
Caput apri defero *(The Boar's head I bring)*
Reddens laudes Domino *(Giving praises to God)*

The boar's head, as I understand,
Is the finest dish, in all the land,
Which thus bedecked with a gay garland
Let us servire cantico *(serve with a song)*
Refrain:
Caput apri defero
Reddens laudes Domino.

Our steward hath provided this,
In honour of the King of Bliss,
Which on this day to be serv-ed is,
In Reginensi atrio *(in Queens' Hall)*
Refrain:
Caput apri defero, Reddens laudes Domino
Caput apri defero, Reddens laudes Domino

9. The Boar's Head with Bay Leaf garland

According to the tale, the tradition began in 1341, inspired by a student who, supposedly, fought off a boar by shoving a book of Aristotle into its jaws and choking it. When served at table, the precious book is replaced by the far more appetising apple in the boar's mouth.

For those of lower status, brawn – chopped pork set in jelly made from a pig's head – is a more affordable version of this dish. Though humble, it was rich and satisfying, a delicacy in its own right.

> **Did You Know?** Those seated at the lowest table in the hall were often served dishes containing offal – the internal organs of a butchered animal, such as kidneys, liver, tripe, lights (lungs), etc. These less-select ingredients were termed 'umbles' – without an 'h' – and frequently put into a pie. This is the origin of our phrase 'made to eat humble pie', meaning to be put in your [lowly] place. The Victorians added the 'h' to humble because they felt only illiterate folk dropped their aitches

Birds of Splendour: Peacock, Swan, and Goose

Birds also featured prominently in medieval Christmas feasts. Swans and peacocks were reserved for the elite and served with theatrical flair. Skinned rather than plucked to keep their plumage intact, roasted and then sewn back into their skins, these birds were presented on a platter in a lifelike pose with flaming tapers in their beaks. They dazzled the eye, if not necessarily the palate.

Apparently, the meat of young mute swans – cygnets – tastes good but, around late December time, the now full grown cygnets moult their youthful grey feathers and take on the handsome white adult plumage. Their beaks change colour, too, from drab to bright orange with the species' 'blackberry' knobble at the head of the beak which is larger in the males. Otherwise, swans of both sexes look similar – to human eyes at least.

10. A roast swan dressed for the table

It isn't only the birds' appearance which changes at midwinter: they change their diet, too, and this affects the taste of their flesh. Therefore, for good eating and to have a bird of maximum size, December was the time to put swan on the menu but you had to catch them just before they took on their dazzling white feathers. This meant that the more gorgeous it looked on the serving dish, the worse it tasted. Only the king or those granted permission could serve swan, it being a royal bird.

Peacocks, rare and costly, were reserved for the most exotic show. But peacock meat isn't particularly tasty and a more palatable bird, such as goose, was often hidden beneath the gorgeous outer skin. However, the peacock meat didn't go to waste. There is a recipe for peacock rissoles, spiced to improve the flavour and garnished with – you've guessed it – more gold leaf.

Bustards were a large bird native to England which became extinct here but have been recently reintroduced to Kent. They are about the size of a turkey, taste good and, apparently, are easy to catch so would have made a great addition to the Christmas table.

The story runs that bustards are curious about everything and will come to investigate anything interesting. To catch one, simply stare at the ground where a bustard can see you, making out that you have discovered something intriguing. The bustard, being nosy, will come to see what you've found and you, with a net hidden but ready behind you, can fling it over the bird and there you have it. Easy! No wonder they became extinct.

> **Did You Know?** Turkeys weren't on the medieval menu because they come from the Americas which hadn't been discovered by Europeans, officially (if you ignore the Vikings) until 1492. It is possible that the notorious Tudor king, Henry VIII, may have been the first English monarch to enjoy a turkey dinner as they were first recorded in 1526, imported by a Bristol merchant, William Strickland. However, by the 1580s, in the reign of Henry's daughter, Elizabeth I, turkeys were definitely the Christmas bird of choice for the wealthy. But in that period, most of our turkeys were imported via Spain and England was at war with the Spaniards. Elizabeth realised that eating turkeys was putting silver into Spanish coffers so she passed a law stating that 'goose is a proper Christmas dish for a patriotic Englishman', and outlawing turkeys! Is our traditional Christmas dinner still illegal?

Ordinary folk celebrated with roasted goose, chicken or capon – a neutered cockerel. These birds were plucked and stuffed with 'forcemeat', an early form of stuffing made with breadcrumbs and herbs before being cooked in their skins. Besides enhancing flavour, the stuffing helped the bird retain its shape and made the meat stretch further.

11. Roast Swan on a pewter charger

Pottages, Stews and Trenchers

Feasting in the medieval period wasn't just about grand centrepieces. Everyday fare, like pottages and stews, was transformed during Christmas into something richer and more plentiful. These thick soups included root vegetables, herbs, pulses and sometimes dried fruits or nuts, providing both nourishment and variety.

Served on trenchers – thick slices of stale bread used as plates – these dishes fed large numbers efficiently. After the meal, the gravy-soaked trenchers were often distributed to the poor, further extending the feast's generosity.

Wassail and Drinking Customs

Wassail, both a beverage and a ritual, was a cherished Christmas tradition with pagan origins. Originally a fertility rite involving apple orchards, wassailing evolved into a toast to good health. The drink – made from ale, apples, spices and honey – was both warming and festive.

A large wooden wassail bowl, decorated with ribbons, would be passed around the room. Toasted bread or croutons floated on top and whoever received one was promised good luck. This communal sharing of the ale reinforced ties of kinship, spread seasonal cheer and is the origin of the more modern idea of 'raising your glasses and drinking a toast'.

The word 'wassail' comes from the Old English 'waes hael' meaning 'be in good health'. Revellers would carry a bowl of spiced ale or, in some traditions, cider, and offer a drink in exchange for hospitality or a coin. But wassailing wasn't just limited to people. In parts of southern England orchard wassailing took place around Twelfth Night. Villagers would parade through the orchards, sing to the trees and pour the drink around their roots to encourage a good harvest. It was a blend of Christian and pagan customs, reflecting the season's deep links with agricultural life. In some regions, especially in the West Country and Kent, the original orchard-wassailing custom continues today but more for fun.

The Church's Dilemma: Celebration vs. Solemnity

While many aspects of medieval Christmas feasting delighted the population, the Church was often caught between approval and dismay. On one hand, the birth of Christ was a holy occasion; on the other, its celebration had absorbed so many pagan elements that it sometimes resembled bacchanalia more than liturgy.

> **A Recipe for Medieval Wassail**
>
> Warm a third of a pint of apple juice with a small pinch of nutmeg,
>
> Add a more generous pinch each of ground ginger and cinnamon and an ounce of sugar.
>
> Stir until sugar dissolves.
>
> Add a pint of ale and a teaspoon of honey and heat through but don't allow to boil.
>
> Add croutons and serve warm with a sprinkle of anise or lemon slices on top.

Despite this tension, the Church adapted and religious services remained central as every feast day began with Mass. But the celebratory elements persisted and, over time, the ecclesiastical authorities had to accept that hospitality and abundance were just as important to the season's meaning as the sacred element.

The Rise of Puritan Restraint

Beyond our medieval time frame but, nevertheless, relevant to our history, by the late sixteenth and early seventeenth centuries, the tone of Christmas feasting began to change. The rise of Puritanism brought serious questioning of the traditional celebrations.

12. A Puritan family at dinner, 17th century

Puritans insisted that every aspect of Christian worship must be based on the words of God, i.e. the Bible, and one precise word was completely absent from that sacred text: 'Christmas'. Therefore, Christmas was man's invention, not God's. Over-indulgence and merry-making were profanities and as Oliver Cromwell's puritanical fellows filled the parliamentary seats at Westminster, they cancelled Christmas – permanently – by Act of Parliament in 1647. Everyone was to attend church and then work as usual: the 25th December was just an ordinary day, not a holiday. There was public outcry against it and a group of London apprentices, who definitely weren't at work, were prosecuted for decorating the local water fountain with a bunch of holly. Traditions such as the pastry Baby Jesus atop a Christmas Pie were regarded as idolatrous and banned.

Folk found ingenious ways to continue celebrating clandestinely. The large Christmas Pie became individual small pies which could be eaten in a couple of bites if the Puritans came calling – no festivities going on here, sir. The actual minced meat element of the pies was eventually phased out in favour of extra dried fruit. Rituals once steeped in symbolism and communal participation became more secular and subdued. Yet the essence of Christmas feasting with its role of bringing society together, an expression of generosity and a celebration of survival in the darkest season could not be destroyed, however hard the Puritans tried. In 1660, with the Restoration of the king, when that famously merry monarch, Charles II, returned to England, Christmas was swiftly re-instated to the calendar.

From ancient pagan festivals to royal banquets, from peasant stews to wassailing bowls, feasting has always been at the heart of the Christmas celebrations. The communal meal allowed folk to forget, however briefly, the harsh winter outside, the great gulf between the rich and the poor and the Church's frown of disapproval. Though the elements of the feasting have changed over time, the idea of gathering together to share and celebrate endures, uniting us with a good dinner.

Chapter 3 – Mysteries, Miracles and Mummers

The Theatrical Heart of Medieval Christmas

13. Mummers Illustration from The Romance of Alexander

A Season of Drama and Delight

Christmas in medieval England was a time of vibrant spectacle, joy and storytelling. It wasn't just about food and drink – it was a festival of the senses, filled with dramatic performances that brought the Bible and local legends to life. In an age before literacy was common or books were widely available, public theatrical performances were vital sources of entertainment, education and religious instruction.

Mystery plays, miracle plays and mummers' performances became part of the community celebrations. These productions, performed in churchyards, marketplaces and streets, filled the dark winter days with colour, noise and spectacle. They blended the sacred with the comic, the solemn with the bawdy and gave medieval audiences a fulfilling Christmas experience.

Sacred Origins: From Altar to Marketplace

14. Joachim's Dream by Giotto

The earliest forms of religious drama in medieval Europe began inside church walls. By the tenth century, monks were staging brief dramatic scenes as visual episodes, such as the Nativity or the Resurrection, to help congregations grasp Christian teachings since few of them were able to read or understand Latin. These scenes were simple and reverent, designed more to illustrate scripture than to entertain.

By the twelfth century, however, these dramatisations had outgrown the confines of the church building. Performed increasingly in the vernacular, whether Anglo-Norman

French or Middle English, and expanding in length and scope to tell the story of the Bible from Genesis to the Last Judgement, the plays began to draw large audiences. This led to them being moved from churches to town squares and public places with lay performers replacing clerics. This marked a turning point: performance as religious instruction became far more a performance for the people to enjoy.

The shift also caused concern among Church authorities: could a comic actor convincingly portray Christ or the Virgin Mary? (Though you have to wonder about a monk playing Eve.) Was it appropriate for the solemn horrors of the Crucifixion to be re-enacted in a rowdy town street? Eventually, the Church distanced itself from the plays but the crowd's appetite for them grew.

What's in a Mystery?

The term 'mystery' as in 'mystery plays' stems from the Latin *mysterium*, meaning religious rites or something which is difficult to understand. However, in medieval towns, trade and craft fellowships or guilds were also accounted to be 'mysteries' because a master had to swear to initiate his apprentice into the mysteries or secret skills of their craft. This is most appropriate because, typically, the plays came to be produced and performed by specific trade guilds. Each guild – such as vintners (wine-merchants), grocers, bakers, goldsmiths, fishmongers, weavers and mercers (dealers in textiles) – took charge of one play as part of the larger cycle of mystery plays. Guilds often selected stories that reflected their profession. Carpenters or shipwrights might perform the story of

Noah's Ark, goldsmiths or mercers tell of the journey of the Kings with royal clothing, crowns and expensive gifts for the Christ Child.

These productions became showcases not only of faith but of craftsmanship and civic pride. Some cycles contained as many as forty or fifty individual plays, performed over several days. Towns like York, Chester, Coventry and Wakefield developed particularly rich traditions, each with its own distinctive cycle, the plays becoming major social and religious festivals, drawing spectators from across the region. In York, the play cycle became so extended, its enactment was moved to the Feast of Corpus Christi in midsummer, instead of the traditional Christmas, because the winter hours of daylight were too short to fit in all the individual pageants to tell the entire Bible story from the Garden of Eden to the Last Judgement.

The Stage Comes to Life: The Pageant Wagons

15. Coventry Mystery Pageant Wagon

Although the medieval towns hosted these marvellous performances what they lacked were permanent theatres to house them, so producers got creative. Mobile, two-level stages, known as pageant wagons, were a defining feature. Pulled from one location to the next, each wagon hosted a different play in the cycle. The upper level served as the performance space, while the lower level housed props and costumes.

Special effects were often impressive and elaborate. Hell scenes featured smoke machines, trap doors, red lighting, thunderous sound effects and grotesque masks to terrify onlookers. Heavenly moments might include angels winched down on ropes from above, accompanied by choirs singing hymns. For a Nativity scene, actors would bring along a live baby, swaddled in rich fabrics. For crucifixions, actors were actually tied to crosses and, in one case, nearly killed by overzealous realism when one, Nicholas, required the attentions of both a physician and a tavern-keeper's wife to revive him. The anecdote doesn't say whose treatment best affected his recovery. These plays turned everyday townscapes into multisensory theatre experiences.

Costumes, Characters and Comic Relief

While early performances relied on actors wearing their everyday garments, costumes evolved over time. Special robes and masks began to distinguish divine figures. For certain characters, costumes were borrowed or cobbled together creatively. There's a record of a goldsmith's wife lending her best gown to a male actor playing Noah's wife – perhaps the first recorded pantomime dame.

The mystery plays managed to strike a careful balance. While they dramatised sacred events, they often wove in physical comedy and satirical jabs at contemporary issues. The audience might watch a devil tempt a merchant with bribes or a priest chastised for greed. These scenes brought Bible stories into relatable, everyday terms – with a healthy dose of irreverence.

16. York Mystery Plays

Did You Know? – Noah's wife, in fact, became a staple of comic relief in England. Hardly mentioned in the Bible or even appearing in continental mystery plays, in many English versions of the Ark story, as the rain begins to fall, Mistress Noah stubbornly refuses to board, preferring to drink and gossip with her friends. The subsequent clash with her husband, Noah, escalates until he and his three sons are forced to frog-march her up the gang-plank, into the Ark. This comedy action gave audiences a humorous interlude and allowed for lively improvisation, continued in English culture to the present with the pantomime dame – that absurd, over-the-top female impersonator beloved by British audiences at Christmas time. As a comedy character, Noah's wife was joined by others such as assorted devils and demons – the more grotesque the better – fools and acrobats and even, supposedly, talking animals.

Miracle Plays and the Cult of Saints

Closely related to mystery plays were miracle plays which focused on the lives and miracles of saints, rather than stories from the Bible. The earliest recorded English miracle play, about St Catherine, was written in 1110 by Abbot Geoffrey of St Albans. Others followed, featuring figures like St Nicholas, St George and St Thomas Becket. The plays celebrated themes of healing, sacrifice, martyrdom and divine intervention. These productions often honoured local saints drawn from regional legends and devotional traditions, helping to foster a sense of local identity and pride. Their structure mirrored that of the mystery plays with pageants and processions. But the tone was often reverent, to ensure the locally worshipped saint was in no way offended, but no less theatrical.

Mummers and the Village Voice

In small, rural communities, where guilds didn't exist and pageant wagons were impractical, a different tradition flourished: mumming. Mummers' plays were informal yet deeply rooted in pre-Christian seasonal rituals and folklore. Performed in homes, taverns or on village greens, they used minimal props and dialogue, relying instead on repetition, rhyme and gesture. The word 'mummer' likely derives from the practice of players wearing masks. Disguises were essential: being recognised was believed to break the magic of the ritual.

The core narrative was usually simple: a hero (often St George) fights and is killed by a villain (a dragon, wicked knight, evil Turk or Saracen), only to be revived by a doctor using a miraculous remedy. Other characters might include Old Man Winter/Father Christmas, Beelzebub and comic fools. In fifteenth-century England, tales of Robin Hood, Maid Marian and their troupe of Merry Men became popular subjects for mummers' plays but Robin wasn't quite the familiar hero we love today who robbed the rich to give to the poor. He was more of a con-man who kept the spoils for himself. But the themes of death, rebirth or resurrection and the turning of the year from old to new were woven into the plays which still had that same ancient, pagan, symbolic power.

Mumming was often accompanied by Morris dancing, another folk tradition with pagan echoes. These group line or circle dances involved rhythmic steps, bells, ribbons and clashing sticks, performed to ward off evil and bring good fortune. Originally part of the winter festivities, Morris dancing has gradually migrated to spring and summer fairs.

17. Morris (Moorish) Men

The dancers traditionally blackened their faces with soot or walnut juice, disguising their identities and preserving their anonymity, just like the mummers and also linked to pagan customs. The name 'Morris' is a corruption of 'Moorish', meaning in medieval English something or someone from North Africa or, more specifically, from Morocco. Like mumming, Morris dancing was both a performance and a ritual, meant to protect the land and people during the coldest season, though whether it truly had any African origins, we don't know. More likely, it was simply that the blackened faces reminded the audience of people with darker skins from hotter lands.

Together, mummers' plays and Morris dancing offered less formal communal delight without the rigid structure of guilds or Church authorities. Their lively storytelling and longevity continue to connect us regardless of class, geography or belief.

Trouble from the Pulpit: Church and Civic Control

As you can imagine, as with Christmas feasting and revelry, not everyone approved of this theatrical exuberance. As mystery and miracle plays grew more elaborate and more irreverent, Church leaders began raising objections. By the thirteenth century, complaints of vulgarity, sexual innuendo and mockery of religious themes were common. Plays were accused of corrupting morals and turning sacred stories into trivial tales. Reformers warned that actors portraying Christ or saints might confuse their roles with reality. Others feared that blasphemy or heresy might creep into performances. The tension between popular entertainment and ecclesiastical authority became hard to ignore.

By the late sixteenth century, several forces led to the decline of medieval religious drama. The Renaissance brought a new wave of secular, classical theatre influenced by ancient Greek and Roman models. Meanwhile, the Protestant Reformation condemned the use of religious imagery in performance, considering it idolatrous and deceitful, with common sinners playing divine roles.

Puritan authorities, in particular, viewed all theatre with suspicion. Mummers were seen as disorderly, their disguises associated with criminality or even rebellion. Mystery and miracle plays were suppressed or faded from favour and with them, sadly, went a rich tapestry of local stories, communal rituals and shared winter revels.

Still, the spirit of these performances lived on. Folk plays survived in oral tradition. Elements of medieval drama influenced later stage genres, from Shakespeare to Victorian pantomime. And in villages, some troupes continued to perform clandestinely or revived traditions when the political climate allowed.

Revival and Remembrance

Today, many of these theatrical customs have been revived as part of our cultural heritage. The York Mystery Plays, for example, are still performed every few years, attracting audiences from across the globe. Mummers' troupes once again march through villages at Christmas, bringing their rhymed couplets, dragon-fights and comic chaos.

18. Flight Into Egypt by Giotto

These revivals are more than just a nostalgic treat. They are living links to a past when theatre was not confined to a stage but spilled into the streets where faith, laughter and storytelling merged to light up the darkest days of the year. Medieval Christmas theatre reminds us that the holiday spirit lies not just in hearty meals and hospitality but in the stories we tell and the joy we share. From pageant wagons to village inns, the heart of Christmas once beat in the rhythm of performance and, thanks to these revivals, it still does.

Chapter 4 – The Twelve Days of Christmas

19. Adoration of the Magi from the Hours of Rene of Anjou

More than just a Song

We often think of the 'Twelve Days of Christmas' as the length of time it takes to get through a quirky song involving lords a-leaping and partridges in pear trees. But in medieval and Tudor England, the Twelve Days were a cornerstone of the festive calendar. They stretched from Christmas Day on 25th December to the eve of Epiphany on 5th January – a dozen days of merrymaking, music, feasting and festivity that linked the religious aspects and the revelry.

This festive period was rooted in Christian tradition but, as we've seen, peppered with older, seasonal customs. The Church celebrated Christ's birth on the 25th, followed by a cycle of feast days including St Stephen's Day (26th December), the Feast of the Holy Innocents (28th December), St Thomas Becket's Feast Day (29th December) and, finally, the Feast of the Epiphany, also known as the Feast of the Three Kings (6th January), which commemorated the visit of the Magi.

For medieval folk, it was a time when the world of work paused. Agricultural routines slowed, law courts closed and social hierarchies loosened. Lords and ladies hosted feasts for their households and in the villages drink flowed freely. Even those of modest means found ways to mark the season.

A Season of Reversal, Boy Bishops and Lords of Misrule

One of the most distinctive features of the Twelve Days was the idea of festive misrule. When we imagine the Middle Ages, we might picture solemn monks in chilly cloisters, stern knights in clanking armour and pious villagers praying for salvation. But peel back the stiff curtain of medieval decorum and you uncover a world that also delighted in comedy and chaotic reversals of order. Nowhere was this more apparent than in the curious traditions of the 'Boy Bishop' and the 'Lord of Misrule' – seasonal figures who turned the world on its head for a brief but raucous time.

20. The Frolic of My Lord of Misrule

In cathedrals and collegiate churches, a Boy Bishop might be elected, symbolically replacing the real bishop for a short time and leading religious services. Or in secular houses, a Lord of Misrule, often a servant, an apprentice or youth, might be appointed to preside over the revels, leading games, plays and crazy activities with mock authority. These reversals served a communal purpose, offering a release of social tensions, encouraging generosity and reinforcing bonds between classes. The Twelve Days were a time to enjoy abundance or at least share what little you had with family, friends and neighbours.

A Boy in a Bishop's Mitre

The idea of placing a child in charge of a cathedral might sound absurd to us today but from the twelfth to the sixteenth centuries, many English and European churches did just that during the weeks of Advent or, more particularly, on the Feast of the Holy Innocents (28th December). The point of the exercise was authority's apology to children, reflecting the awful biblical event when King Herod commanded his soldiers to slay all male children under two years old in the hope of killing the Christ Child – a possible future rival for Herod's throne – amongst them. It was also a reminder to those in authority that they were still capable of making terrible mistakes and pride was a sin. A choirboy, elected by his fellow choristers, would be dressed in episcopal robes and crowned as the Boy Bishop, just as the humble Christ would rise to glory. Even kings could be mocked safely and symbolically when a choirboy in a too-big mitre stood in the bishop's seat.

This wasn't just fancy dress for the sake of spectacle. The Boy Bishop would perform many of the symbolic functions of his adult counterpart, leading processions, delivering sermons (often ghost-written by the clergy, though occasionally witty or cheeky) and overseeing special masses. His tenure lasted from St Nicholas's Day (6th December), the patron saint of children, to Holy Innocents'

Day, commemorating the massacre of infant boys in Bethlehem.

Cathedrals like Salisbury, Hereford and York were particularly fond of the custom where elaborate ceremonies marked the boy's brief elevation. The Boy Bishop might process through the town with a retinue of 'canons', also played by boys, collecting small donations and blessings. At St Paul's Cathedral in London, records show the practice being actively encouraged throughout the fifteenth century with the dean and chapter providing funds for the boy's vestments and special feasts in his honour.

The practice was popular but, like so many Christmas traditions, not universally loved. In 1542, Henry VIII, never known for his sense of humour when it came to religion, issued a proclamation banning the tradition, viewing it as irreverent and disruptive. Yet, it briefly returned under the Catholic restoration of Mary I, only to be finally extinguished with the rise of the Protestant Elizabethan church.

The Lord of Misrule: When Servants played Kings

If the Boy Bishop represented the Church's moment of sanctioned mischief, the Lord of Misrule was his secular counterpart, presiding over the Yuletide revels in manorial halls, noble households and even royal courts.

The custom had deep roots, echoing the Roman Saturnalia during which slaves could swap roles with their masters, wearing their togas – symbols of citizenship and authority – turning the garments inside out and causing merry havoc. In medieval England, the Lord of Misrule – sometimes called the Abbot of Unreason in Scotland – was elected to supervise the festive follies from Christmas to Twelfth Night.

His duty consisted of causing chaos. The Lord would be crowned with mock regal dignity, dressed in bright, often absurd, clothing and given licence to command games, plays and lewd entertainments. He might order a 'parliament of fools' or require that everyone speak in rhyme or invent ludicrous court titles for his entourage. Household order was inverted: servants mocked their masters, the solemn became silly and laughter was compulsory. There are shadows of Old Man Winter here.

21. Old Man Winter

Records from noble households, such as those of the Howard family at Framlingham or the Nevilles of Raby Castle, describe the Lord of Misrule in action. One account tells of him arriving at dinner, riding on a horse made of barrels, demanding the steward serve wine while hopping on one leg. In London, the Inns of Court held elaborate masques and mock trials, all under the Lord's riotous rule.

Games were an important part of Christmas fun and some are familiar to us today, like chess, draughts (checkers) and noughts-and-crosses (tic-tac-toe). Other games have names we recognise but were played quite differently and with little regard for health and safety. One example is blind man's buff in which one player is blindfolded and then disorientated by being spun around several times. The other players, who are not blindfolded, have fun by calling out to the 'blind man' and dodging away from him. Any player touched or caught by the blind man takes on the blindfold, although sometimes the blind man must guess the identity of his captive before the blindfold is removed (if the guess is wrong, the captive is released and the game continues).

But in medieval times blind man's buff was an adult game and the blindfolded player was struck and buffeted – hence 'buff' – by the other players. Also, if the game was played in the great hall with its central open fire, scorched feet were a definite possibility. Indoor tug-o'-war carried similar risks, the more so, if the participants were drunk on an excess of wassail.

Board games were popular for quieter moments – and safer. 3-men's, 6-men's or 9-men's morris were more intricate forms of noughts-and-crosses played on boards of complicated design though sometimes simply scratched into a stool or window seat with any kind of improvised counters. Fox-and-geese was a strategy game for two players and games involving luck and the throw of dice, such as hazard, drew spectators who were eager to wager bets on who would win. Games recognisable to us, such as skittles, quoits, bowling and stilt-walking could add to the festive fun and were often insisted upon by the Lord of Misrule to add to the chaos.

In Henry VIII's court, the Lord of Misrule took on a glittering, theatrical grandeur. The courtier, George Ferrers, famously filled the role, organising revels that included elaborate pageants, mock jousts and even satirical plays lampooning court politics. Henry, ever a fan of display, seems to have approved, so long as he was never the butt of any of the jokes. But again, the party couldn't last.

> **Did You Know?** – Games and gambling – generally banned for common folk throughout the year – might well be permitted during the Twelve Days. Dice, cards (introduced from the continent late in the fifteenth century) and other diversions filled the long dark evenings and, just for the season, even normally frowned-upon activities might be temporarily tolerated, at least by the more lenient authorities.

The Puritans, always suspicious of idleness and revelry, viewed the Lord of Misrule as a dangerous emblem of sin and waste. Under Oliver Cromwell's Commonwealth, both Christmas and Misrule were banned altogether. Though the monarchy and many of these customs were restored in 1660, they never quite returned with their previous enthusiasm.

The Meaning behind the Madness

Why did these traditions of mockery flourish for so long? In many ways, the answer lies in their acts of subversion. Medieval society was hierarchical and deeply conscious of status. God had determined your place, whether king or dong-farmer – remember them? – and there you must be content to remain. But the Church also understood the benefits of an occasional symbolic release from this rigid structure. For one short season, rules could be broken, safely. The Boy Bishop was a reminder that the lowly could rise and the Lord of Misrule ensured that laughter and liberty could flourish, however briefly, but all would be restored to good order and everyone return to their rightful place come Epiphany. It was, perhaps, a way for society to let off steam without threatening the system.

These crazy inversions were also about community, engaging entire parishes or households. Even peasants could enjoy watching their betters mocked by fools while noble lords delighted in playing along with a joke that, for once, wasn't at the expense of the poor.

Echoes Today

Though the Boy Bishop and Lord of Misrule are no longer fixtures of a British Christmas, echoes survive. In some cathedrals, like Hereford, ceremonial Boy Bishops have been revived as historical pageantry. Modern pantomimes and Christmas crackers retain that spirit of festivity and reversal. And you might argue that figures like the Christmas pantomime dame or the office party prankster are distant descendants of the Lord of Misrule's reign.

In a world still bound by social hierarchies and unwritten rules, perhaps we could use a bit more of that medieval mischief. Just a touch, mind you, before the bishop returns to his rightful seat and the Lord of Misrule is packed away until next year.

22. Salisbury's Cathedral's Boy Bishop

The Crowning Feast: Twelfth Night and Epiphany

Twelfth Night marked the close of the festive Twelve Days. This was the evening of 5th January, the night before the Feast of the Epiphany celebrating the arrival of the Three Kings to present their significant gifts to the Christ Child. It was traditionally one of the grandest parties of the season. A special Twelfth Night cake was often baked, a rich, spiced fruit cake containing a hidden bean or coin. Whoever found it in their slice became the 'king' or 'queen' for the night, presiding over festivities with their 'court' – the last role reversal of the celebrations.

In noble households, masques and plays were common on Twelfth Night and gifts might be exchanged, though these were often modest tokens. In some parts of Europe, this was the main day for Christmas gift-giving, rather than Christmas Day itself. Surprisingly, in medieval and Tudor England, the morning of 1st January was the time for royal gift receiving and, hopefully, giving. A book of instruction for the household of Edward IV [r.1461-83] describes how the king would receive courtiers to present their gifts in his bedchamber whilst barefoot in his night robe, standing on a foot sheet. In this case, the gifts were expected to be spectacular – jewellery, golden goblets, bolts of silks, even horses or the deeds to a property, depending on how desperately you needed to curry favour with the monarch at the time.

The Road to Candlemas

While the Twelve Days officially ended with Epiphany, the Christmas season didn't come to a close entirely. In fact, the full festive cycle extended all the way to Candlemas, celebrated on 2nd February. In religious terms, this marked the Feast of the Presentation of Christ in the Temple, also known as the Purification of the Virgin Mary.

23. Presentation of Christ in the Temple

In medieval and Tudor England, Candlemas was seen as the definite end of the Christmas season. It was a time of transition, from festivity to the more solemn season of Lent which would often begin shortly after, although the date varies considerably, depending on when Easter will fall in a given year. Candlemas was also a day connected to the gift of Light with the gradual return of longer hours of daylight. Candles would be brought to church for special blessing and carried in procession. They symbolised Christ as the 'Light of the World' and people often kept a few of these blessed candles at home to use in times of illness or storms.

Households traditionally took down their Christmas decorations at Candlemas – not on Twelfth Night, as we tend to do today. Greenery, such as holly and ivy, which had adorned homes for over a month, was ceremonially removed, often with a song or prayer. Superstition warned against keeping decorations up beyond Candlemas in case it brought misfortune.

A Season of Contrast and Continuity

From Christmas to Candlemas, the medieval and Tudor festive season was an evolving blend of sacred and secular, Christian and folk traditions. It was a time when kings might dine beside peasants in symbolic feasts, when lively songs rang out beside solemn hymns and when candles flickered in halls, churches and cottages alike.

Today, while we rarely keep the season going until February, echoes of these traditions remain in the form of carols, cakes and communal festivities. And perhaps there's something to be said for revisiting the rhythm of this extended celebration, allowing more room for reflection, warmth and light in the darkest part of the year.

> **Did you know?** Plough Monday, was the first Monday after Epiphany (January 6th) and marked the traditional start of England's farming year.

Chapter 5 – The Spirit of Christmas Giving

24. The Adoration of the Magi, C.13th

Sacred Origins: The Magi and Meaningful Offerings

The festive season today is a blur of wrapping paper, shopping sprees and hopeful wish lists but the roots of Christmas gift-giving stretch back centuries, deep into biblical symbolism, feudal customs, royal theatrics and humble village rituals. From gold-laden palaces to frost-covered hovels, the act of giving has always been central to the midwinter season. So, let us take a cheerful stroll through the centuries, tracing how the tradition of Christmas presents evolved, from sacred gestures to sentimental surprises.

The custom of Christmas giving finds its spiritual beginnings in the story of the Magi, the Three Wise Men who followed a star to Bethlehem or, by late medieval times, the Three Kings. Their titles may change but the gifts they brought to the Christ Child – gold, frankincense and myrrh – remained the same. These were not childish playthings for a baby but deeply symbolic tributes: gold for a king, frankincense for worship and myrrh for mourning, signifying a royal birth worthy of praise but foreshadowing the ultimate sacrifice. Unlike us, medieval Christians didn't swap gifts under a decorated tree but the example of reverent giving, inspired by the Magi, lingered.

Power, Politics and Presents: Medieval Royal Customs

In medieval Europe, gift-giving wasn't about pleasant surprises or sentimental thoughts. It was concerned with ceremony, strategy and showmanship. Among royalty and the nobility, seasonal gifts often arrived not on Christmas Day but at New Year, as we saw with King Edward IV earlier. These offerings were not so much personal: rather they were tributes meant to secure favour, demonstrate loyalty and reinforce the social hierarchy. Monarchs expected them, courtiers planned them and everything was recorded in meticulous detail – who gave what to whom and how the act was reciprocated, if, in fact, it was. Sometimes, the Tudor monarchs especially would snub a giver, refuse or return the gift later and give nothing in exchange – then you knew you were in serious trouble.

> **Did You Know?** – On New Year's Day 1562, Queen Elizabeth I received presents from her courtiers. Almost all the dukes, marquises and earls gave her purses containing money – most generous was the Archbishop of Canterbury who gave her a red silk purse with £40 in half [demy] sovereigns. But some people were more creative in their gifts. Her Secretary, William Cecil, gave her a silver-gilt dish on a stand decorated with mother-of-pearl, a matching ink well with a crystal in the lid on a silver-gilt tray with two boxes for 'duste' – that would probably be one for pounce or chalk dust, the other for fine sand, both used to sprinkle on wet ink to dry it. Also a penknife with a silver-gilt handle for cutting quills into shape, a carved bone seal, again with a silver-gilt handle and mount and, for her majesty's leisure moments, twenty-four silver-gilt gaming counters. More imaginative still: Sir John Strump gave the queen two greyhounds – a Tudor emblem – one black and white and one described as 'fallow'. Lady York, knowing Elizabeth's fondness for sweets, gave the gift of three sugar-loaves and a barrel of sucket – that is sugar syrup. Lady Carew gave her a black silk smock with collar and ruffles decorated with gold and silk embroidery and Lady Fitzwilliam gave a petticoat of purple satin and gold sarcenet with two gold and silver-embroidered borders fringed with gold, silver and silk.

In 1377, King Richard II's court festivities dazzled over 10,000 guests. The scale of giving was grand with gold, jewels, exotic textiles and even estates changing hands. Similarly, Henry VIII and Elizabeth I used Christmas gifts as tools of diplomacy and to parade their dominance. One year, Anne Boleyn gave her lover, King Henry, a shirt she had sewn and embroidered with her own hands. In this case, it was a deeply intimate present as the king would wear it next to his skin. He reciprocated with a glittering array of diamonds. No gift was casually given: everything, from the gift's material to its timing, was choreographed for full effect.

25. Alexander enthroned, receiving gifts sent by Darius

Lords and Land: Gifts on the Manor

While monarchs played politics with gold and gowns, a different sort of exchange unfolded on country estates. Lords were expected to show generosity to those who worked their land, especially during the Twelve Days of Christmas. Seasonal tokens might include: a goose or a side of bacon, ale or mead served in the great hall or blankets, tools or cloth for bedding or clothing. Tenants might return the gesture with eggs, hand-carved trinkets or a bundle of firewood but these weren't always optional and could be demanded as part of the tenancy agreement, bound by custom and duty, part of the social contract. A generous lord earned respect; a mean one risked complaint or, worse, rebellion.

Humble Celebrations: Peasant Traditions and Simple Joys

For the poor, gift-giving wasn't about prestige. It was about community and comfort. Children received small tokens, perhaps a few nuts, an apple or a wooden toy carved by a family member. Villagers might share baked goods or pots of preserved fruit or pickled vegetables. Offering a warm hearth or a cup of mulled ale was a gift in itself as with the popular tradition of wassailing we heard about earlier. In the countryside, gifts weren't wrapped but they were baked, sung, poured or shared by the fire. And while they didn't sparkle like the royal jewels, they carried the warmth of real human feelings.

The Role of the Church: Charity and Christian Duty

While the nobility exchanged gold and gossip and peasants shared bread and ale, the Church championed charity. Inspired by both scripture and the example of St Nicholas (see chapter 7), almsgiving during Christmastide was not just encouraged, but expected. The poor might receive food, clothing or firewood, distributed by monasteries, parish churches or wealthy households. One such tradition was the Christmas dole, when villagers queued for bread and ale outside their local lord's hall. In towns, children sang carols for sweetmeats or coins. These acts weren't just kindness; they were good for the soul. Christian teaching held that charity could redeem a person's sins and gain divine favour.

Continental Cheer: A European Medley of Giving

Across mainland Europe, Christmas gift-giving took on regional flavours with traditions tied to agriculture, folklore and the Church calendar.

26. La Befana, Italy's Christmas Witch

In France, the New Year's tradition of *étrennes* saw adults and children receive small presents, often coins or sweets. In Italy, the Epiphany (6th January) brought *La Befana*, a kindly witch who rewarded good children and left a lump of coal for the mischievous. Germanic folklore featured characters like *Frau Holle* or *Perchta*, wintery goddesses who inspected homes and left blessings (or mischief) depending on cleanliness and behaviour. Food and cloth were offered in return for household luck. These customs were part of agricultural ritual, ensuring fertility, protection and prosperity as the year turned.

Thoughtful Tokens: Georgian and Early Victorian Years

By the eighteenth century, British Christmas traditions were beginning to change. While New Year was still the time for adult exchanges, children increasingly received small gifts on Christmas Day itself. These were 'token gifts': maybe a puzzle, a sugar plum or a small book. Often tucked into stockings, they reflected growing domesticity and changing views of childhood – in medieval times, children were mostly regarded as small adults and occasional play was a pastime for young and old, so childhood was nothing special.

The middle class, now up-and-coming in wealth and influence, embraced Christmas as a time for personal, sentimental giving. Commercialism stirred – shops offered special 'Christmas novelties' for the first time – but the emphasis was still on meaning rather than how much money was spent.

Meanwhile, aristocratic households continued to gift generously, especially to staff and servants but within set expectations. It became traditional to give the items in 'Christmas boxes' on 26th December, rewarding the servants for their extra efforts to make the previous day special. That's how 'Boxing Day' came about – nothing to do with fisticuffs and split lips and everything to do with a bottle of fine malt whisky for the butler and a pair of woollen stockings for the scullery maid. Just like in medieval times, the scale of giving reflected your place in the social order.

A Tradition That Keeps Evolving

Today's Christmas giving may be worlds away from medieval feasts or a few coins in a slipper but the threads of tradition still run deep. Whether it's a diamond pendant for the queen, a wooden toy carved by a village blacksmith or a carefully chosen book tucked under the tree, the message is the same: 'I thought of you'. Across time and class, from royalty to rural villagers, the act of giving has meant generosity, obligation, love and community. And while styles and customs have shifted, the heart of Christmas giving has always been about connecting with others.

Across Europe, gifts are given on various dates according to different traditions: the Feast of St Nicholas (6th December), New Year's Day or the Feast of the Three Kings (6th January). In Britain we have compromised, sharing presents on Christmas Day (25th December).

From the sacred gifts of the Magi to the home-brewed wassail of peasant villages, from courtly strategy to childhood wonder, Christmas gift-giving tells the story of a society and its values. So next time you're tying a ribbon or slipping something into a seasonal gift bag, remember that you're part of a long, rich tradition, one in which a gift, no matter how small, is never just a thing. It's a gesture of generosity: a legacy of light in the darkest season.

Chapter 6 – Echoes of Joy

27. Illuminated Music Manuscript

When Carols Began

Long before Mariah Carey and Slade took over the festive airwaves, the sound of carols echoed through medieval towns and countryside halls in a very different fashion. The tradition of Christmas carolling has its roots in medieval Europe and it wasn't always about the Nativity or snow-covered rooftops. The word 'carol' comes from the Old French *carole* which originally referred to a circle dance accompanied by singing and wasn't necessarily connected to Christmas at all.

These early carols were festive songs sung at all kinds of communal gatherings, whether celebrating the seasons, the harvest, weddings or religious feast days.

By the twelfth century, however, carols began to be associated with events in the Christian calendar, particularly with the celebration of Christ's birth. This transformation marked the beginning of the Christmas carol as we know it today. Unlike the solemn Latin chants used in formal church services, carols were lively, tuneful and often sung in the vernacular language, making them a popular entertainment in homes, marketplaces and on village greens.

Medieval Melodies and Yuletide Revelry

During the medieval period, music played an important role in both sacred and secular life. Christmas was one of the high points of the Christian year and, as we've seen, communities found myriad ways to mark the occasion through feasting, games, pageantry and, of course, singing. While the Church focused on more liturgical forms of music, such as plainsong sung by monks and choristers, carols were sung by everybody and found their way into more informal religious gatherings and community celebrations.

Carols in this period were often narrative in nature, telling stories from the Bible or celebrating figures such as Mary, Joseph and the shepherds. They frequently included refrains to encourage participation, making them suitable for communal singing. We heard earlier about the well-known 'Boar's Head Carol', dating back to the fourteenth century, which was sung at the presentation of the boar's head during feasts and how the lyrics merge elements of pagan winter feasting and Christian symbolism.

> **Did You Know?** – Minstrels and wandering musicians played a vital role in spreading carols across towns and regions. These performers would travel from manor to village, entertaining crowds with a mixture of songs, stories and instrumentals. During Christmas, their repertoires often turned to carols which could be both devotional and light-hearted. In this sense, carolling became a kind of oral tradition, preserving stories and customs through generations.

Carol Singing: From the Hearth to the Church

As the centuries passed, carol singing became more firmly associated with Christmas and increasingly found a place within churches and homes. By the late medieval period and into the early modern era, as we've seen, communities often staged elaborate Christmas Pageants and Mystery Plays which incorporated music and song to great effect. These performances helped to embed carols further into seasonal observances.

We don't have much information about many early carols. However, we have these few words but, sadly, no music for this brief song written in English by Richard Smart who lived from 1435-77:

Welcome, Sir Christmas,
Welcome to us all,
Both more and less,
Come near, Nowell!

Definitely a festive flavour here and 'Sir', like 'Father', was a correct form of address for a Catholic priest in medieval times. The phrase 'Both more and less' refers to folk of both high birth and those of lesser status. 'Nowell' is the English spelling as Smart wrote it, not our more common modern French spelling, 'Noël'. The tune was probably a spirited one, suitable for a circle dance. Another carol, referred to as 'Gaudete' (pronounced gow-day-tay) for which we have both music and lyrics – in Latin this time – was written down in the Elizabethan period but was likely sung much earlier. It has a lively, merry melody and was revived by the folk-rock group Steeleye Span in the 1970s and continues to be sung today. Here is the refrain:

> Gaudete! Gaudete! Christus est natus *(Rejoice! Rejoice! Christ is born)*
>
> Ex Maria virgine. Gaudete! *(Of the Virgin Mary. Rejoice!)*

Another early carol, first written down in 1534, is the 'Coventry Carol'. Despite its Tudor date, the song was performed as part of a Mystery Play: 'The Pageant of the Shearmen and Tailors' which was performed in Coventry as early as 1392, so it is probably far older. The play tells the harrowing story of the Massacre of the Innocents in which King Herod orders all male infants under the age of two in Bethlehem to be killed. The accompanying carol takes the form of a lullaby sung by three women, mothers of the doomed children.

A single version of the lyrics was noted down by Robert Crow in the reign of Henry VIII, shortly before Mystery Plays and other forms of religious theatre were banned as the Protestant Reformation advanced in England. Crow had been manager of the Coventry pageants for twenty years or more and payments to him are recorded for playing the part of God in the 'Drapers' Pageant', for making a hat for a 'pharysye' [Pharisee], for mending and making other costumes and props as well as writing new dialogue and copying out the 'Shearmen and Tailors' Pageant', adapting and editing older material. When religious changes caused the suppression of the plays, Crow's prompt book, including the songs, survived, only to be destroyed in a fire at Birmingham Library in 1879. Fortunately, a transcription made of it in 1825 was more fortunate so we have the text of the carol today.

Within the pageant, the sad carol is sung by three women of Bethlehem who enter on stage with their children after Joseph is warned by an angel to take his family and flee to Egypt:

> Lully, lullay, thou little tiny child,
> Bye bye, lully, lullay.

> O sisters two, how may we do
> For to preserve this day
> This poor youngling for whom we sing,
> Bye bye, lully, lullay?

> Lully, lullay, thou little tiny child,
> Bye bye, lully, lullay.

> Herod the king, in his raging,
> Chargèd he hath this day
> His men of might in his own sight
> All young children to slay.

Lully, lullay, thou little tiny child,
Bye bye, lully, lullay.

That woe is me, poor child, for thee
And ever mourn and may
For thy parting neither say nor sing,
Bye bye, lully, lullay.

Lully, lullay, thou little tiny child,
Bye bye, lully, lullay.

28. The Olivetan Master Monks

Churches, which had previously been cautious about songs which weren't sung in Latin, began to include carols in their celebrations, particularly during the festive Twelve Days of Christmas. These were not only opportunities for worship but social events and music made them all the more memorable. It wasn't uncommon for villagers to sing carols, going door-to-door, in the hopes of receiving a warm drink, a coin or some food in return – a tradition that included 'wassailing' (see Chapter 2).

The Decline and Revival of Carols

Like other festive traditions, carols saw a sharp decline during the Puritan era in the seventeenth century. Under

Oliver Cromwell's rule, Christmas celebrations were banned as being too indulgent and lacking any biblical foundation. Carolling, along with feasting and festive games, was discouraged or totally forbidden. While some folk continued the tradition behind closed doors, the idea of joyful community music and dance suffered.

It wasn't until the nineteenth century that Christmas carols saw a major revival, thanks to the Victorian enthusiasm for rediscovering medieval customs. Romanticism and antiquarian interest in folklore played a role with writers and musicians collecting, publishing and arranging traditional carols that might otherwise have faded into obscurity.

One of the most influential collections of the time was *Christmas Carols, Ancient and Modern*, compiled in 1833 by William Sandys. It included many familiar carols such as 'God Rest Ye Merry, Gentlemen' and 'The First Nowell'. This publication, along with the popularisation of Charles Dickens' novella *A Christmas Carol*, helped to revive public enthusiasm for festive singing. The Victorian ideal of Christmas, centred round the family, generosity and tradition, found the perfect companion in carol singing. Though the accompanying element of dance has mostly disappeared, it survives in the traditional circle dance, the 'Hokey-Cokey'. If you don't know it, it's probably to view on YouTube.

Churches began holding formal carol services, such as the now-famous 'Festival of Nine Lessons and Carols' first held at King's College Chapel, Cambridge, in 1918. These services helped to bridge the gap between sacred and secular traditions, combining scripture readings with carol singing in a structured format that remains popular to this day.

European Traditions and Regional Flavours

While English-speaking traditions dominate much of what we consider modern carolling, Europe has a rich and varied heritage of its own. In France, for instance, the *noël* was a popular form of carol dating back to at least the fifteenth century. These songs often mixed folk melodies with devotional texts and were widely sung in village squares and churches.

In Germany, the tradition of Christmas music included both *Weihnachtslieder* (Christmas songs) and more solemn hymns. Martin Luther, the German monk who set the Protestant Reformation in motion in 1517, encouraged the use of music in worship and even composed carols, helping to lay the foundation for a Lutheran musical tradition that included both choral and congregational singing.

> **Did You Know?** – Martin Luther may also have invented the Christmas tree when he took a bough from a fir tree into church and decorated it with candles to remind the parishioners that Christ's birth brought the light of redemption into the world. Notoriously, Luther also broke the rules that Catholic monks, priests and nuns must remain celibate when he set up home with a nun, married her and they had children!

O Tannenbaum ('Oh Christmas Tree') and *Stille Nacht* ('Silent Night') are just two examples of how Germanic traditions deeply influenced the modern carol list.

In Italy, the *zampognari* (bagpipe players from the mountains) would descend into towns during the Advent season, playing traditional carols in the piazzas. These pastoral songs, with their imagery of flocks and shepherding, echoed the Nativity story and brought a rustic charm to city streets.

A Living Tradition

Today, Christmas carols continue to thrive, sung in schools, churches, town centres and living rooms across the UK and beyond. They link us not only to our own childhood memories but to generations past who stood in candlelit halls or frosty fields, raising their voices in song.

What began as medieval dance tunes and seasonal storytelling evolved into devotional hymns, community rituals and cherished family customs. And while the modern carol might be accompanied by a brass band or a downloaded playlist, its essence remains timeless: to celebrate, to share and to bring people together through music.

29. *14th-Century Gradual (Introit Gaudeamus omnes)*

Chapter 7 – Old Man Winter, Saint Nicholas and Father Christmas:

30. Old Man Winter

The Evolution of a Festive Icon

As we wrap up our exploration of medieval Christmas traditions, we turn to one of the most enduring and beloved figures of the season: Father Christmas – also known in different times and places as Old Man Winter, St Nicholas or Santa Claus. Today's jolly, red-suited gift-bringer is the result of centuries of evolution, drawing from ancient mythology, Christian tradition and folklore across Europe. To fully understand this complex figure, we must explore his three primary incarnations:

Old Man Winter: The Wild Spirit of the Cold Season

Long before Christian missionaries reached Northern Europe, winter was personified as Old Man Winter, a powerful, untamed figure embodying both the brutal chill and the spirited revelry of the season. In Germanic and Viking traditions, this spirit was often associated with Woden (or Odin) who was believed to lead the Wild Hunt through the stormy skies in the dead of winter. Odin rode an eight-legged horse and was believed to bestow small gifts on those who respected him, inspiring later tales of sky-travelling gift-bringers.

Old Man Winter wasn't malevolent but he wasn't exactly benevolent either. Cloaked in a frosted bearskin complete with toothed jaws and carrying a club or staff, he represented winter's extremes of cruel weather yet also communal feasting to excess and celebration. Anyone who showed a lack of enthusiasm for the rituals of survival and joy: drinking, singing, storytelling and making merry in defiance of the dark, was likely to feel the blunt end of his club.

This figure's ambiguity – both festive and fearsome – reflected the worldview of early pagans. The Yule season, now part of the broader Christmas calendar, was rooted in these winter observances. Fires were lit, songs were sung and offerings left by the hearth to placate or please the visiting spirits. Old Man Winter represented the year's dying phase, a time when boundaries between worlds were thin.

St Nicholas: A Bishop of Generosity and Legend

As we've seen in earlier chapters, as Christianity spread across Europe, the Church sought to reframe popular seasonal customs into religious observance. The Church considered the popular figure of Old Man Winter a most unsuitable representative of the midwinter season with his gluttony and violent tendencies but the traditional idea of generous gift-giving fitted well with Christian teaching. A new representative was required and the Church decided upon a suitable candidate from the fourth century AD: St Nicholas of Myra (in modern day Turkey), famed for his anonymous acts of charity.

31. St Nicholas

The most enduring tale tells how Nicholas was born of wealthy parents who died when he was young, leaving him the sole inheritor of their riches. But Nicholas decided to enter the Church and give his fortune to the poor. He was down to his last three bags of gold when he overheard a father complaining that his three daughters would never be able to marry because he couldn't afford dowries for them.

That night, Nicholas crept to the girls' bedroom window and tossed in a bag of gold which landed in the eldest daughter's stocking where it hung to dry by the fire. After she was happily wed, Nicholas repeated the secret gift-giving for the second girl. But, when it came to the third daughter, he found the bedroom window closed so climbed onto the roof and dropped the last bag of gold down the chimney. Again, it landed in her stocking. What a relief! Nicholas had finally disposed of all his unwanted gold!

Though some details, such as the chimney, were added much later – there were no chimneys in the fourth century – the story of a secret benefactor giving to the needy became central to the saint's reputation. Celebrated on 6th December, Nicholas' feast day became an occasion for secret surprises, such as small sweets or coins, often left in shoes or stockings. Though separate from Christmas proper, the traditions eventually blurred together.

By the fourteenth century, children in the Low Countries, Germany and parts of England were placing shoes by the fire on 5th December, hoping for fruit, coins or small trinkets. The gifts weren't lavish – they were magical. They arrived secretly, rewarding good behaviour, delivered by a figure who, somehow knew who had been good or bad. Even after the Protestant Reformation dimmed saintly traditions, the spirit of Nicholas survived, evolving into Father Christmas in England and Christkind in other Protestant regions. The emphasis remained on anonymous winter giving and the sense of an enchanted reward.

Despite his broad appeal, St Nicholas remained primarily a religious figure: a bishop in ecclesiastical robes, representing divine generosity rather than festive indulgence. But his popularity led to his becoming the patron saint of the poor, children and unmarried girls in particular as well as pawnbrokers – who still use three golden balls as their symbol, representing his three bags of gold. He's also the patron of bakers, bankers, brewers and brides; coopers (barrel-makers), jurors, perfume makers, prostitutes, robbers – yes, even criminals have their own saint – sailors, scholars, students and travellers in general. Russia and Greece have Nicholas as their especial patron as well so he must be a very busy saint.

The Green Knight

In an anonymous Middle English poem, *Sir Gawain and the Green Knight*, we meet King Arthur and his knights celebrating New Year's Eve at Camelot when the eponymous Green Knight arrives to disrupt the festivities.

32. The Green Knight

This terrifying figure is green from head to foot, rides a green horse and carries a fearsome axe. He proposes a deadly game: one of Arthur's knights may behead him with his axe but the Green Knight will return the same blow a year and a day later. Nobody is keen to accept the challenge even though it seems unlikely there can be any retribution once the Green Knight is slain.

Reluctantly, Sir Gawain accepts and beheads the Green Knight who, miraculously, stands, retrieves and reattaches his head, mounts his horse and rides away, reminding Gawain of his promise to allow the blow to be returned next year. The rest of the poem tells of Gawain undergoing tests of loyalty and chivalry on his quest to find the Green Chapel where the final confrontation will take place on the next New Year's Day.

Gawain sets off to find the Green Knight and, during his journey, stays at a castle. The lady of the castle attempts to seduce him and offers him a magical green girdle to keep him safe. Gawain resists temptation but accepts the girdle secretly. The Green Knight reveals he is the lord of the castle and that the entire ordeal was a test of Gawain's courage, chivalry and honesty. When Gawain kneels to suffer the fatal cut, he receives only a nick on the neck, punishment for dishonestly keeping the girdle a secret. Otherwise, he is accounted honourable by the Green Knight, though Gawain sees it as a failing. He returns to Camelot, bearing the green girdle as a symbol of his imperfection but his fellow knights treat him as a hero and take to wearing similar green girdles.

Sir Gawain represents a good but fallible Christian – brave, chivalrous but not entirely honest – but it's the Green Knight who personifies Nature and earlier pagan rites. He is the Old Year which dies on New Year's Eve to begin afresh and resurrected on New Year's Day: Nature returned to life. If you want to steep yourself in medieval Christmas celebrations, *Sir Gawain and the Green Knight* is a good read.

Father Christmas: The English Spirit of Merriment

In England, another figure emerged, not saintly but secular. Father Christmas – or Sir Christmas – began as the embodiment of holiday cheer, a personification of good fellowship rather than divine grace. He inherited aspects of Old Man Winter – but not the club, luckily – appearing in festive pageants and literature by the fifteenth century. Dressed in green or earth-toned robes adorned with holly and ivy, Father Christmas was depicted as a portly, cheerful elder who encouraged feasting, laughter and open-hearted hospitality. He was a seasonal symbol, not a gift-giver, and his focus was on having a communal good time. His arrival marked the Twelve Days of Christmas, when households hosted generous meals and welcomed strangers.

33. The earliest image of Father Christmas, 1658

Though his image shifted over time, Father Christmas maintained his identity as a promoter of merriment. During the Puritan rule of Oliver Cromwell, when Christmas was suppressed, Father Christmas became a symbol of resistance, appearing in pamphlets and satires lamenting the loss of traditional festivity. After the monarchy was restored in 1660, Father Christmas regained popularity. He was a nostalgic figure of revelry and warmth, a character in masques and plays, reflecting England's enduring love of seasonal cheer.

A New Synthesis: Santa Claus in the New World

The modern Santa Claus is a blend of Old Man Winter's wild magic, St Nicholas's generous heart and Father Christmas's festive warmth. The transformation began in earnest with Dutch settlers in New Amsterdam (now New York), who brought with them the tradition of Sinterklaas – a phonetic evolution of 'St Nicholas'.

Sinterklaas was already a fusion of sacred and folkloric traits: he rewarded good children, carried a staff and travelled across the sky and over rooftops. In time, his image merged with English notions of Father Christmas and American storytelling. By the early nineteenth century, writers and illustrators helped reshape this character. Washington Irving mentioned him in his satirical histories. Clement Clarke Moore's 1823 poem, *A Visit from St Nicholas* (''Twas the Night before Christmas') gave him reindeer, a sleigh and a chimney-centric delivery method.

In Moore's poem, Santa becomes smaller, rounder and more jolly – a significant departure from the solemn bishop. This cheerful figure soon captured the public imagination. The nineteenth-century American illustrator Thomas Nast further developed the image in *Harper's Weekly*, depicting Santa with a workshop, assistant elves and a North Pole residence.

By the twentieth century, marketing confirmed the look. Coca-Cola's holiday advertisements, starting in the 1930s, standardised the red suit, fur trim and rosy cheeks, features that had previously varied. These campaigns reached millions, crystallising a universal image of Santa that echoed but did not duplicate, his earlier forms.

Echoes of the Past in the Present

Despite commercialisation, today's Santa Claus carries deep historical resonance. His red robes may evoke Coke ads but they also recall the bishop's vestments of St Nicholas. His jollity and hearty welcome stem from Father Christmas while his nocturnal travels through the winter sky hark back to Woden's spectral Wild Hunt. More than an advertiser's invention, Santa represents a figure rewritten over generations yet always rooted in midwinter's eternal themes: hope, warmth, generosity and renewal. His evolution from pagan spirit to bishop to folk hero illustrates the adaptability of seasonal traditions.

Santa's longevity lies not just in his magical flights or sacks of toys but in the values he represents: compassion, abundance and community. In this way, he carries forward the essence of every winter festival, from Saturnalia to the Yule fires to Christmas stockings.

As long as we gather to celebrate, to share stories and to give freely, the spirit behind Old Man Winter, St Nicholas, and Father Christmas will live on – they are the enduring Spirit of Medieval Christmas: ever ancient, ever new.

34. St Nicholas still delivering gifts

Table of Images

1. Bringing home the evergreens; Illustrated London News, 1957

2. Old Man Winter, Norse representation

3. Dice Players from Osteria della Via di Mercurio, Pompeii

4. Anglo-Saxon carving, Wirksworth, Derbyshire; photo, G. Mount

5. Winter Solstice at Stonehenge, Wilts, 2022; photo Skynews

6. Banquet of Richard II, Jean de Wavrin Chroniques d'Angleterre c.1480; Royal MS 14 E IV BL

7. Goose Pie; London by Gaslight

8. Boar's head brought to the table; Granger Historical Picture Archive

9. The Boar's Head with Bay Leaf garland; photo, G. Mount

10. Roast Swan centrepiece, Nordic Museum, Stockholm

11. Roast Swan on Pewter Charger; source unknown

12. A Puritan family at dinner, 17th century woodcut; Historic UK

13. Mummers Illustration, The Romance of Alexander Ms. 264, fol. 21v; Bod

14. Joachim's Dream, Giotto-Scrovegni, c.1300; Musei Civici di Padova

15. Coventry-mystery-pageant, engraving by David-Gee-1825; Beinecke Library, Yale

16. York Mystery Plays 1992; yorkmysteryplays.org

17. Morris Dancers 2008; thefranandfronkinshow, Flickr

18. Flight Into Egypt by Giotto, c.1300; Cappella degli Scrovegni, Italy

19. Adoration of the Magi from the Book of Hours of Rene of Anjou Egerton 1070 f.34v BL

20. The Frolic of My Lord of Misrule, 1900; Cassell's History of England

21. Old Man Winter, wind-blown pareidolia, 2014; attributed to Debbie Love, Flickr

22. Boy Bishop, 2014, Salisbury Cathedral; photo, Ash Mills

23. Presentation of Christ in the Temple, Sherbrooke Missal c.1310; MS 15536E NLW

24. The Adoration of the Magi, Psalter loose leaf, c.1240; Getty

25. Alexander receiving gifts, Roman d'Alexandre, c. 1420; Royal 20 B XX, f. 24r BL

26. La Befana, Italy's Chrstmas Witch; famiglieditalia

27. St Peter and St Paul, attributed to Ludovico Gaci, Italy 1489; NGA USA

28. The Olivetan Master of Monks, Lodi Choir Books, Italy c. 1430; Beinecke MS 1184, Yale

29. Graduale Aboense, hymn book of Turku, Finland. C14th, Helsinki University Library

30. Map of the Winds (detail) Geographicus Anemographica, Jannson-1650

31. St. Nicholas by Andrija Raičević, 1641; Church of the Holy Archangels, Sarajevo

32. The Green Knight, source unknown

33. The Examination and Tryal of Old Father Christmas, 1658; Folger Shakespeare Library, USA

34. Early twentieth-century Dutch greetings card of Saint Nicholas

Rear Cover: Les très riches heures du Jean Duc de Berry (Ms. 65) – Musée Condé à Chantilly, France

These images are all considered to be in the Public Domain and are widely available online under wiki Creative Commons, or elsewhere, and are included here in good faith in the spirit of sharing knowledge and information.

Index

A Christmas Carol 69
A Visit from St Nicholas 79
Aelfred, King of Wessex 13-15
Aethelberht, King of Kent 13, 15
Anglo-Saxons 9, 12-13

Bible 13, 30, 32, 34-5, 37-8, 64
Blancmange recipe 20
Boar's Head/carol 19, 22-3, 64
Boxing Day 61
Boy Bishop 44-7, 51-2

Candlemas 53-4
Carols 54, 59, 63-5, 68-70
Charles II, King of England 31
Chester 37
Chippenham 14-15
Christianity 8, 10, 12-14, 16-18, 73
Christmas Carols, Ancient and Modern 69
Christmas Day 13, 44, 52, 56, 61-2
Christmas Eve 112
Coventry 35, 66-7

Dickens, Charles 69

Edward IV, King of England 52, 56
Elizabeth I, Q. of England 26, 57
Epiphany 14, 44, 51-53, 60
Father Christmas 9, 39, 72, 75-80
Feast of Three Kings 14, 44, 51-53, 60
Feast of Holy Innocents 44, 46-7

Forme of Cury cookery book 19-20
France 60, 70

Games 48-50, 64, 69
Germany 70, 75
Gold 56-9, 74-5
Gold leaf 21-22, 26
Guthrum, Viking leader 14-15

Henry III, King of England 18
Henry VIII, King of England 26, 47, 50, 57, 66
Hereford 47, 51

Italy 60, 70

Jesus/Christ 11, 18, 21, 29-30, 34-5, 40, 46, 52, 54, 56, 66
John, King of England 18

Kent 13, 15, 26, 28
King's Coll Chapel, Cambridge 69

Lord of Misrule 45, 47-8, 50-1

Magi 21, 43, 55, 62
Martin Luther 70
Midwinter/Middewinter 7-8, 10-1, 13, 17, 25, 55, 73, 80
Mince/Christmas Pie 20-1, 30
Minstrels 65
Mistletoe 11-12
Moore, C.C. 79

Morris Dancing 39-40
Mummers/Mumming 32, 38-41
Mystery/Miracle Plays 32, 34, 37-8, 40-1, 65-6

New Amsterdam/New York 79
New Year 56-7, 60-62, 76-7
Noah's Wife 36-7

Odin 73, 80
Old Man Winter 8-9, 39, 48, 72-3, 78-80
Pantomime 36-7, 41, 51
Plough Monday 54
Protestant Reformation 41, 66, 70, 75
Puritans 30-1, 41, 50, 68, 78

Queens' College, Oxford 22

Raedwald, King of East Anglia 15
Reformation 41, 66, 70, 75
Richard II, King of England 17, 19, 57
Robin Hood 39
Romans 10, 12, 22

Sandys, William 69
Santa Claus 9, 15, 72, 79-80
Saturnalia 10, 17, 47, 80

Sinterklaas 79
Sir Gawain and the Green Knight 76-7
St Augustine 12-13
St George 38
St Nicholas 38, 46, 59, 62, 72-5, 79-81
St Stephen's Day 46
Stonehenge 8, 16

Three Kings/Wise Men 21, 44, 52, 56, 62
Turkeys 26
Twelfth Night 28, 48, 52, 54

Umble Pie 24

Victorians 24
Vikings 9, 15, 22, 26

Wakefield 35
Wassail 28, 31, 49, 59, 62, 68
Wassail recipe 29
Wild Hunt 9, 73, 80
Winter Solstice 8, 10, 16-7
Woden/Odin 9, 12-3, 73

York 37, 41, 47, 79
Yule/Jul/Yule log 9, 47, 64, 73, 80

Meet the Author

Toni Mount is a best-selling author of both medieval fiction and non-fiction books, with over 30 published titles. Her book *Everyday Life in Medieval London* was named 'Best History Book of the Year' in the year of its release and became an Amazon bestseller. Her internationally popular Sebastian Foxley medieval murder mystery series has earned over 15 million page reads on Kindle Unlimited.

An historian and experienced educator, Toni holds a Master's degree from the University of Kent, a first-class Batchelor's degree, with Honours, and diplomas in European Humanities and English Literature and Creative Writing from the Open University, as well as a PGCE from the University of Greenwich. She is a member of the Richard III Society's Research Committee and contributes regularly to history magazines and blogs. She teaches history and offers a range of unique online courses at MedievalCourses.com. She lives in Kent with her husband Glenn and has two grown-up sons.

Also by Toni Mount

Echoes from History
The Medieval Housewife and Women of the Middle Ages
Richard III King of Controversy
The History of Medieval Gravesend
Medieval Christmas

Amberley Publishing
Everyday Life in Medieval London
Dragon's Blood and Willow Bark: the mysteries of medieval medicine
The Medieval Housewife: & Other Women of the Middle Ages
Medieval Medicine: Its Mysteries and Science
A Year in the Life of Medieval England
The World of Isaac Newton

Pen & Sword Books
How to Survive in Anglo-Saxon England
How to Survive in Medieval England
How to Survive in Tudor England
How to Survive in Ration-Book Britain

MadeGlobal Publishing
The Death Collector (A Victorian Melodrama)
The *Sebastian Foxley* Medieval Murder Mystery Series

Online courses at Medievalcourses.com
Everyday Life of Medieval Folk
Heroes and Villains
Richard III and the Wars of the Roses
Warrior Kings of England – The Plantagenet Dynasty
England's Crime and Punishment through the Ages
The English Reformation: A religious revolution
The Roles of Medieval and Tudor Women

Medieval Christmas | Toni Mount